rather_chicago_

eat. shop. explore > discover local gems

researched, written and photographed by anna h. blessing

toc

neighborhoods

EAT

90 miles cuban cafe
big jones
birrieria reyes de ocotlán
black dog gelato
chickpea
chilam balam
crisp
crust
doughnut vault
floriole
great american
cheese collection
great lake
hoosier mama pie company
hot doug's
kuma's corner
lillie's q
little branch cafe
longman & eagle
lovely
mana food bar
maria's packaged goods &
community bar
marigold
merlo on maple
nana
nightwood
old oak tap
olivia's market
perman wine selections
perennial virant
pleasant house bakery
province
rootstock
ruxbin
sarah's candies
sepia
simone's
southport grocery and café
takashi
taxim
the bluebird
the coffee studio
the depot american diner
the fish guy market
the whistler
urbanbelly
xoco

SHOP

abraham lincoln book shop
apartment number 9
asrai garden
bari zaki studio
branca
brimfield
deliciously vintage
dovetail
elements
foursided
greer
hadley
june blaker
kokorokoko
merz apothecary
michael del piero good design
morlen sinoway atelier
optimo hats
p. 45
patina
penelope's
p.o.s.h.
post 27
robin richman
roslyn
scout
soutache
space 519
sprout home
state street salvage
the sweden shop
tula
urban remains
uusi
zap props

notes
about
chicago

rather *chicago* EDITOR >

Anna H. Blessing has authored scads of
eat.shop books and also contributes to
Design*Sponge and other publications with
the BBB Craft Sisters

Something's up in Chicago. There's beer and pizza, sports and politics—but NOT as usual. For example, when I talk politics, I'm talking President of the United States. And as for this town's traditional fare? Hot Doug's dogs, Great Lake's pizza and Kuma's Corner's burgers are so popular that you are almost guaranteed a queue with a bunch of hungry hounds itching for these re-imagined Windy City classics.

Out-of-towners have been lining up for large-scale eateries and name brand shops in Chicago for years, but it's a new phenomenon that people are seeking out off-the-beaten-path local treasures. Travelers and locals alike are paying serious attention to this city's outstanding local shops and eateries. If Barack Obama, Frank Gehry and Renzo Piano have played a part in creating a Chicago buzz, it's no doubt the fantastic local businesses you'll find in this book that have kept the excitement building.

Outside of the world of eating and shopping, here are a few of my favorite things in Chicago:

1 > The River: Amazing bridges, a fascinating history, fantastic city views and an expanded riverwalk with outdoor cafes. And you thought the lake was great.

2 > The Alfred Caldwell Lily Pool: It's hard to narrow down what I like best about expansive Lincoln Park, but this hidden haven has to be it.

3 > Architecture: I'm sweet on SOM's Hancock, Goldberg's Marina City and Mies' LSD buildings, but this is just a snippet—the architectural wonders of Chicago are endless.

4 > Millennium Park: I never tire of it—tennis on the courts, a swing around the shiny bean, a walk through Lurie Garden, or a meander over the snaking walkway. And now there's a new bridge to the gorgeous new Modern Wing of the Art Institute.

it's all about...

exploring locally

*discovering a sense of place
behind the veneer of a city*

*experiencing what gives
a city its soul through its
local flavor*

rather EVOLUTION

If you are thinking this book looks suspiciously like an *eatshop guide*, you're on to something. As of October 2011, the *eatshop guides* evolved into **rather** to give readers a more vibrant experience when it comes to local eating and shopping. It's all about what you'd **rather** be doing with your time when you explore a city—eat at a chain restaurant or an intimate little trattoria devouring dishes the chef created from farm fresh ingredients? You get the idea.

USING **rather**

All of the businesses featured in this book are first and foremost locally owned, and they are chosen to be featured because they are authentic and uniquely conceived. And since this isn't an advertorial guide, there's no money exchanging hands • Make sure to double check the hours of the business before you go, as many places change their hours seasonally • The pictures and descriptions for each business are meant to give a feel for a place, but please know those items may no longer be available • Our maps are stylized, meaning they don't show every street • Small local businesses have always had to work that much harder to keep their heads above water, and not all the businesses featured will stay open. Please go to the **rather** website for updates • **rather** editors research, shoot and write everything you see in this book • Only natural light is used to shoot and there's no styling or propping.

restaurants >
$ = inexpensive $$ = medium $$$ = expensive

Go to **rather.com** to learn more

where to lay your weary head

for more hotel choices, visit >

chicagohotel.net

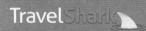

the james hotel
55 east ontario street
312.337.1000 / jameshotels.com
standard double from $259
restaurant: david burke's primehouse
bar: jbar
notes: a focus on good design and art with kiehl's
products in the rooms

public chicago
1301 north state parkway
312.787.3700 / publichotels.com/chicago
standard double from $150
restaurant: pump room
notes: iconic ambassador east hotel transformed
by ian schrager

dana hotel and spa
660 north state street
888.301.3262 / danahotelandspa.com
standard double from $199
restaurants: aja
bar: vertigo sky lounge
notes: a mod yet tranquil hotel

hotel felix
111 west huron street
312.447.3440 / hotelfelixchicago.com
standard double from $150
restaurant: elate
notes: the city's first green, leed-certified hotel

w chicago > city center
172 west adams street
312.332.1200 / starwoodhotels.com
standard double from $260
restaurant: ipo
notes: reliably stylish hotel

sax chicago
333 north dearborn street
312.245.0333 / thompsonhotels.com
standard double from $130
restaurant: bin 36
bar: crimson lounge
notes: chic boheme style right on the river

more eating gems

*these businesses appeared in
previous editions of eat.shop chicago*

longman toggle

angel food bakery
athenian room
avec
bistro campagne
blackbird
bongo room
bonsoiree
bourgeois pig
bricks
chalkboard
cippolina
coco rouge
cru café and wine bar
custom house
de cero
fat willy's rib shack
feed
flo
fonda del mar
fox & obel
frontera grill
green zebra
hai yen
hotchocolate
intelligentsia
irazu
jane's
japonais
jin ju
juicy wine company
(now 694 wine & spirits)
la creperie
le bouchon
lula café
matchbox
milk & honey café
mirai sushi
mixteco grill
mk
moody's pub
naha
old fashioned donuts
pasticceria natalina
pastoral
ping pong
ras dashen

red hen bread
rockit bar & grill
smoque
sultan's market
sushi wabi
sweet mandy b's
tac quick
the bleeding heart bakery
the brown sack
the goddess and grocer
the map room
the original rainbow cone
the silver palm
tocco
tre kronor
tweet
valhalla
victory's banner
volo

more shopping gems

these businesses appeared in
previous editions of eat.shop chicago

a new leaf
alcalas
american science
blake
eskell
europa books
gem
grow
habit
i.d.
ikram
jake
kara mann
komoda
larkspur
lulu's
modlife
nina
ouest
primitive
quake collectibles
red dog house
revival
rotofugi
rr#1 chicago
saint alfred
salvage one
stitch
tangerine
the boring store
the house of glunz
the left bank
the painted lady
the red balloon co.
the t-shirt deli
twosided
up down tobacco
urban remains
white chicago
wolfbait & b-girls
wright

gold coast
river north

eat

shop

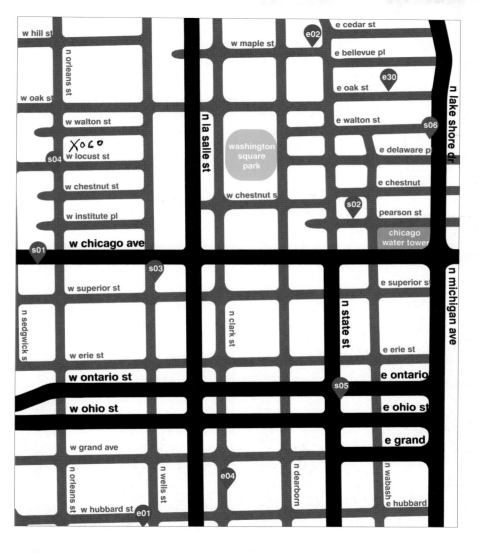

abraham lincoln book shop, inc.

civil war and presidential book shop

357 West Chicago Avenue
Between Orleans and Sedgwick
(River North) *map S01*
Brown Line: Chicago
312.944.3085
www.alincolnbookshop.com

mon - wed 9a - 5p thu 9a - 7p
fri 9a - 5p sat 10a - 4p
online shopping

Yes. Please: *every lincoln history book you could imagine, limited edition set of sandburg's lincoln, 1863 map of battle of gettsyburg, civil war history books*

Pretty soon, they'll probably start calling Illinois the "Land of Obama." But until then, Abe's still got seniority here, and if you need to know anything about him, this is the place to come. Okay, so he isn't the sole subject of the **Abraham Lincoln Book Shop**; you can find items that involve some of his fellow presidents and a war or two— but for the most part, Abe's the main attraction. Browse a little, learn a little, sightsee (some incredible historical documents hang on the walls here), and feel pride for one of our greatest presidents.

branca

incredible interior design shop

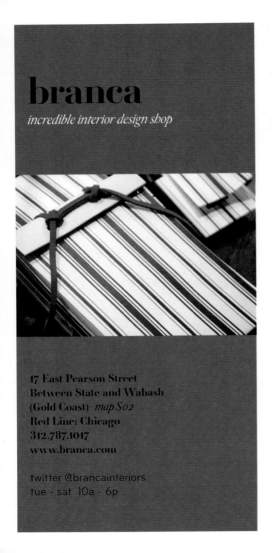

17 East Pearson Street
Between State and Wabash
(Gold Coast) *map S02*
Red Line: Chicago
312.787.1017
www.branca.com

twitter @brancainteriors
tue - sat 10a - 6p

Yes, Please: *gold agenda book, etched garnet lowball glasses, gilt faux bois candleholder, log stool with gold leaf finish, shagreen tray, natural pine candlesticks*

If you're an interior design mag junkie like me, you've no doubt come across spreads on houses where Alessandra Branca has designed the interior. Her work is jaw-droppingly, out-of-this-world stunning. I tend to devour these pages, holding them up to my nose so I can see each glorious detail. I want to crawl inside the pages to touch the fabrics and sit on the furniture. While I've never toured one of these fantasy houses, I can certainly tour her store, **Branca**. Even taking home just a little something from here makes me feel like I have a bit of Alessandra's magic in my own home.

doughnut vault

doughnuts, with a little bit of glitz

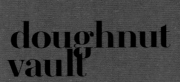

400 1/2 North Franklin Street
Corner of Kinzie
(River North) *map E01*
Brown Line: Merchandise Mart
www.thedoughnutvault.tumblr.com

twitter @doughnutvault
tue - fri 8:30a - until out of doughnuts
sat 9:30a - until out of doughnuts
treats
$ cash only. first come, first served

Yes, Please: *$1 coffee, doughnuts: gingerbread stack, buttermilk old fashioned, glazed (chestnut, vanilla, chocolate), coconut, dreamsicle, pineapple, apple cider, double chocolate*

Half an hour before the Doughnut Vault opens, there is a line outside. Businessmen, girls in their running clothes, all gathered together to wait for the just-made goodies inside. Although there are only three kinds of doughnuts on the menu, these line-dwellers may spend 30 minutes talking about what to order once they get inside. And inside is small but grand: an old bank vault converted to a sugary sanctuary, blasting Beastie Boys (or Snoop Dogg or Naughty by Nature, depending on the day) and filled with racks of soft, doughy treats. Call it a craze, call it hype, but a good idea is a good idea, and a brilliantly executed one is the **Doughnut Vault**.

elements

a go-to spot for gifts

Ages ago, Elements first opened on Wells. Then they moved to Oak, which is when I became aware of them. It was a beautiful place that I would gaze into, but it seemed to call out to a more moneyed and mature audience. Then **Elements** moved back to Wells and it went through a total transformation. Though it maintained its previous beauty, it also became, dare I say, edgier—and with the addition of a coffee bar. I became quite besotted. Now this is one of my go-to places to get gifts for friends and family of any age. And I sometimes gift myself a little something.

june blaker

*high style novelty items, jewelry
and curiosities*

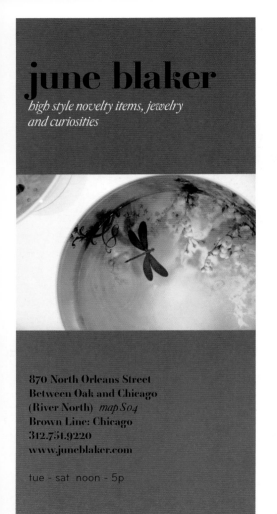

**870 North Orleans Street
Between Oak and Chicago
(River North)** *map S04*
**Brown Line: Chicago
312.751.9220
www.juneblaker.com**

tue - sat noon - 5p

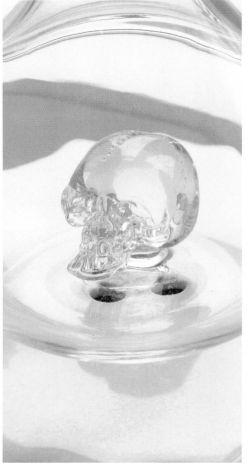

Yes, Please: *batucada bracelets, samantha goldberg
jewelry, lumen candles, redshift leather, commes des gar-
çons wallets, esque studio glass, brelli*

Ever since June Blaker first saw "Blade Runner" she dreamed of and searched for the glowing umbrella—a lit up shaft with a black hood—seen in the movie. Decades later, she found them, and they became one of the quirky items she stocks at her eponymous store. Recently, however, the umbrella company folded, and her hunt began anew. This is the persistence of June—and it shows in everything here. Whereas there's an incredible eclecticism on display, nothing is random. You know that June has carefully hand-picked everything right down to the smallest mounted butterfly.

merlo on maple

upscale authentic bolognese

46 West Maple Street
Between Dearborn and State
(Gold Coast) *map E02*
Red Line: Clark
312.335.8200
www.merlochicago.com

twitter @marlomaple
daily 5:30p - close
dinner
$$$ reservations recommended

Yes, Please: *any cocktail that david the bartender suggests, 01 nebbiolo "ghemme" dessilani rsv., bresaola, taglioline paglia e fieno, tonno rosato, budino di amaretti*

As I decided which eating spots to include in this book, I used the Giampaolo and Silvia litmus test. Though you might think I consider my publisher, friends and family or locals while making up my list, truth be told, I had two people on my mind: the brilliant restaurateurs behind **Merlo on Maple**. Would the places I chose pass muster with them? I guess you might ask why I would care. Because **Merlo** to me is perfection. When I sit at the bar here for dinner, the experience is perfect from beginning to end—including, of course, Sylvia's always delicious food.

p.o.s.h.
european flea market style

**613 North State Street
Between Ontario and Ohio
(River North)** *map S05*
**Red Line: Grand
312.280.1602
www.poshchicago.com**

mon - sat 10a - 7p sun 11a - 5p
online shopping

2ᶠ50

Yes, Please: *hotel silver, vintage mahjong tiles,
etched filigree french glasses, vintage french bingo numbers,
ceramic bistro match strike, cast iron piggy bank*

If I were awarding prizes for fan favorite in this book, P.O.S.H. would win hands down. Everyone I know who has set foot in this store has become instantly infatuated with it. Karl Sorensen manages to keep things always changing and has a knack for displaying his European flea market finds in a way that makes you feel like you are right there in Paris or Piccadilly bargaining for these desirable items yourself. And what's even better is you don't have to figure out how you're going to carry home a dozen vintage glasses in your carry-on.

sarah's candies

chocolate shop and café

70 East Oak Street
Between Michigan and Rush
(Gold Coast) *map E03*
Red Line: Lake
312.664.6223
See website for other locations
www.sarahscandies.com
twitter @sarahscandies
mon - sat 8a - 6p sun 10a - 6p
treats
$ first come, first served

Yes, Please: *intelligentsia coffee, chai tea latte,*
carrot cream cheese muffin, royaltines, mom's fudge brownie,
toffee sugar cookie, chocolate covered marshmallows

A while back I moved away from the Gold Coast, and while I'm loving my new neighborhood, I'm bemoaning the fact that I am no longer a short walk away from **Sarah's Candies**. It's bad news that I can't make a quick run over for a coffee and a few crunchy bunches of royaltines or a slab of chunky rocky road, which both require serious will power to stop devouring. But the good news is that since my walk has now more than tripled, I am justified in eating a chocolate-covered marshmallow or perhaps a peanut butter s'more, or even better, both!

space519

*inspired home goods, accessories
and clothing*

**900 North Michigan Avenue
(In the 900 Shops)
Between Walton and Delaware
(Gold Coast)** *map S06*
**Red Line: Chicago
312.751.1519
www.space519.com**

twitter @space_519
mon - sat 10a - 7p sun noon - 6p

Yes, Please: *wm. j. mill & co. sailmaker bags, rgb nail
polish, sachajuan haircare, the hill-side shirts, 19 4t pants,
illesteva sunglasses*

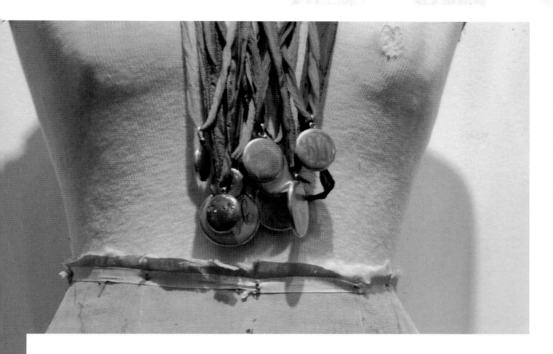

Everyone loves a reinvention, right? If Madonna and Gaga can reinvent again and again, why can't we? Shop owners Lance Lawson and Jim Wetzele are doing just this at their new endeavor **space519**. The shop is replete with totally desirable things for home and self. The pair is constantly remixing the store, focusing on a new motif to inspire the shop every few months and using that theme to totally redesign and restock the mini home showroom in the space. Not even the Queen of Pop can launch a reinvention with that frequency and success.

XOCO

tortas, churros and chocolate

449 North Clark Street.
Corner of Illinois (River North) *map E04*
Brown/Purple Lines: Merchandise Mart
312.334.3688
www.xocochicago.com

tue - thu 8a - 9p fri - sat 8a - 10p
breakfast. lunch. dinner
$-$$ first come, first served

Yes, Please: *chocolate café con leche, churros, mexican vanilla-sour cream coffeecake, ahogada torta, choriqueso torta, xoco salad, shortrib red chile soup*

I am the youngest of three sisters, so when **Xoco**, meaning "little sister," opened as the third Frontera sibling (**Topolobampo** and **Frontera Grill** being the others), I had an immediate affinity for it—nevermind that I would be attracted to just about any place that Rick Bayless opened. Just as there is always a bit of competition between siblings, it's hard to pick which of this trio I love the most with their different charms. But **Xoco's** freshly ground hot chocolate and churros make me think that the little sister has leaped to the top of my list. Aren't little sisters the best?

lincoln park

old town

eat

shop

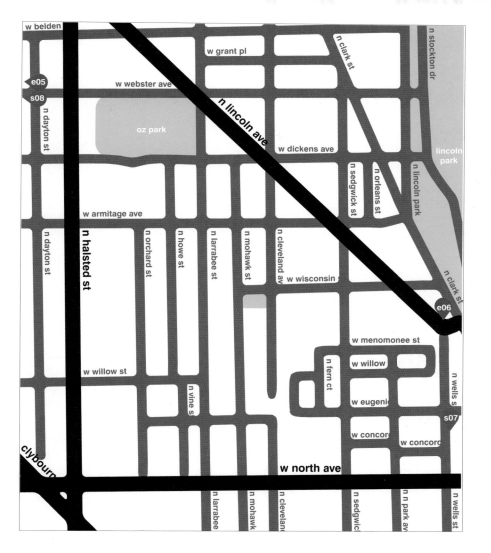

floriole

french café and bakery

1220 West Webster Avenue
Corner of Magnolia
(Lincoln Park) *map E05*
Brown/Purple/Red lines: Fullerton
773.883.1313
www.floriole.com

twitter @floriole
mon 8a – 2p tue – fri 7a – 5:30p
sat 8a – 5:30p sun 8a – 4p
breakfast. lunch. coffee/tea
$$ first come, first served

Yes. Please: *rare tea cellar teas, ramp & goat cheese quiche, tartines, clafoutis, cornmeal lime cookies, lemon lavender pound cake, canelé, sea salt caramels*

The first thing you notice about Floriole is the quality of light in the space. It's otherworldly, bright even when it seems dreary outside. The second thing you notice about **Floriole** is the air. It's perfumed with just-baked bread, caramelized canelé and fresh-from-the-oven quiche. With origins at Green City Market, **Floriole** moved indoors to this permanent space but managed to capture the airy lightness of being outdoors. They brought with them all of the farm fresh ingredients, and their menu offerings taste homey, classic, fresh, and comforting all at once— like you would imagine eating on a family farmstead years ago.

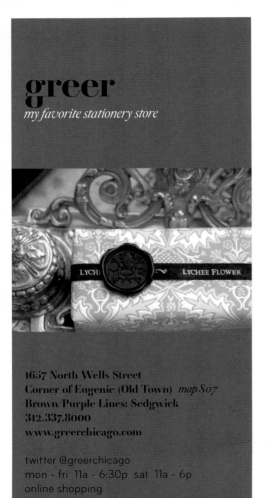

greer
my favorite stationery store

1657 North Wells Street
Corner of Eugenie (Old Town) *map S07*
Brown/Purple Lines: Sedgwick
312.337.8000
www.greerchicago.com

twitter @greerchicago
mon - fri 11a - 6:30p sat 11a - 6p
online shopping

Yes, Please: *greer civilettes portable thank you notes, rifle paper co. botanical stationery set, angela adams address book, mateo ilasco everything, elum cards*

CIVILETTES®
for Spontaneous Regrets ™

I've tried. I really have. But it's just not possible. I can't show you how great this store is with just three small photographs. Sure, I can give you a sense of **Greer**, but you have to actually come here, touch things, look closely, and walk around and around and around, each new circle revealing desirable items that you didn't notice on the first circle. To try to sum up **Greer** in just three measly shots, like I said, is impossible. I'm thinking I need a full book to show the brilliance and beauty of this special stationery boutique. I'll get working on that.

hadley
smart design for smart babies

4205 West Webster Avenue
Between Racine and Magnolia
(Lincoln Park) *map So8*
Purple/Red Lines: Fullerton
773.883.0077
www.hadleybaby.com

tue - fri 11a - 7p sat 11a - 5p
sun 11a - 4p
online shopping. registries

Yes, Please: *playsam planes, netto collection cribs, cariboo folding bassinet, plan toys dancing alligator, vilac calder kangaroo, netto polar bear rocker, bloom loft highchair*

Do you ever wonder what great creative minds like Frank Lloyd Wright or Henry Moore played with when they were babies or what type of crib they slept in? Do you speculate about what could have happened if they had Alexander Calder pull toys or Kapla building blocks at their disposal? We'll never know, but you can surround your mini Matisse with great design at an early age with cool stuff from **Hadley**, where you'll not only find toys, but kids' essentials like high chairs and strollers. Kids and creativity go hand-in-hand, and **Hadley** is there to help!

perennial
virant

local food, all year long

1800 North Lincoln Avenue
Corner of Wells (Old Town) *map E06*
Brown Line: Sedgwick
312.981.7070
www.perennialchicago.com

twitter @perennialchi
daily 5 - 10p sat - sun 10a - 2:30p
dinner, brunch
$$$ reservations accepted

Yes, Please: *remember the maine forest cocktail, crispy carnaroli, lamb sausage fazzoletti, smoked dietzler ribs, fresh whole wheat pappardelle, ed's organic cornmeal cake*

One of the sad things about today's modern world: we are losing our craftsmen. Sure we're quick with a keypad and good with our thumbs, but where have all of the trades gone? I'm exaggerating, but there is a lot of "how-to" knowledge that we're losing as a whole. Thankfully chefs are preserving a lot of these skills, and a chef like Paul Virant may singlehandedly start a canning and preserving revolution. Once you taste the fresh local flavors he preserves to use year round, you'll want to know the tricks of his trade. Hopefully his wall of jars inspires you to can, but if you can't, eat at **Perennial Virant**.

lakeview

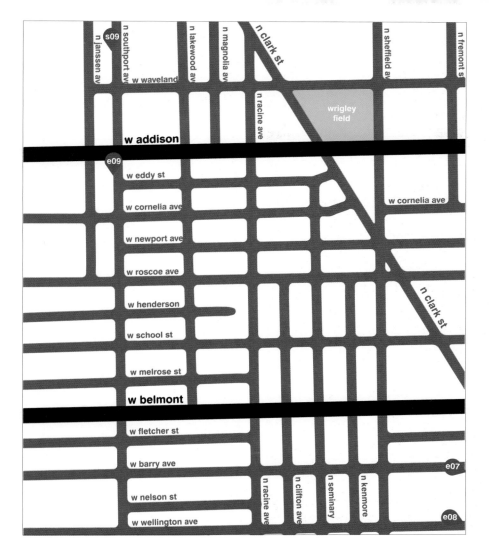

chilam balam

farm-fresh cocina mexicana

3023 North Broadway Street
Between Barry and Wellington
(Lakeview) *map E07*
Brown/Purple/Red Lines: Belmont
773.296.6901
www.chilambalamchicago.com

twitter @chilambalamchi
tue - thu 5 - 10p fri - sat 5 - 11p
dinner, byob
$$ reservations accepted

Yes, Please: *escolar crudo with green garlic chimichurri, chicken albondigas, grilled pork ribs in honey-pasilla sauce, beef brisket threads in adobo sauce, hibiscus flan*

In Chicago, whether you've bussed, valeted, or cooked for Rick Bayless, his name is like gold. Chef Chuy Valencia may be a Bayless protégé, but the gold rush happening to **Chilam Balam** has everything to do with what he has created on his own. **Chilam Balam** is on the tips of the tongues of everyone these days looking for incredible flavor and ingredients in a super laid-back space. The restaurant—literally underground a few steps down from the street—feels like a secret dinner spot that only a few are privy to. Luckily this is one dining establishment where there seems to be enough gold to go around.

crisp
modern korean

2940 North Broadway Street
Between Wellington and Oakdale
(Lakeview) *map E08*
Brown/Purple Lines: Diversey
773.697.7610
www.crisponline.com

tue - sun 11:30a - 9p
$-$$ first come, first served
lunch. dinner

Yes, Please: *grape juice drink with sac, tahitian treat,
crisp bbq korean fried chicken, seoul sassy korean fried
chicken, the buddha bowl*

I like a lot of heat in my food. This need for spice runs in the family, as my brother's special drink of choice is vodka on the rocks loaded with hot peppers, pickles and onions. This is the drink version of getting smacked around. So when I tried the classic crisp BBQ fried chicken at the highly addictive modern Korean joint **Crisp**, I asked for a little extra heat. My taste buds were not disappointed. Since then, I've been eyeing the suicide sauce bird—but I'm thinking I'll have to take it to go, so I can partner it with a flaming vodka or two.

southport grocery and café

upscale grocery and café

3552 North Southport Avenue
Between Addison and Cornelia
(Lakeview) *map E09*
Brown Line: Southport
773.665.0100
www.southportgrocery.com

twitter @southportgrocer
mon - fri 7a - 4p sat 8a - 5p sun 8a - 4p
grocery. breakfast. lunch
$$ first come, first served

Yes, Please: *lavender lemon mimosa, bloody mary, stuffed french toast, grilled coffee cake, the cupcake pancakes, the cheese box, lolla-rosa beet salad, chocolate toffee scone*

Here's the proof that Southport Grocery makes drool-worthy food: the place is swarming with pregnant women. Though the bun in the oven crowd sometimes has some off-kilter cravings, most of the time they want satisfying, healthy, homey food. This pretty much sums up **Southport**. And I probably don't even need to mention their famous cupcake, which at this point probably has a city holiday named after it, though I will mention the cupcake pancakes, a downright genius idea. You know you are going to wake up tomorrow craving some of those.

tula

effortlessly sophisticated women's clothing

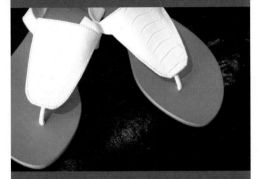

3738 North Southport Avenue
Between Grace and Waveland
(Lakeview) *map S09*
Brown Line: Southport
773.549.2876
www.tulaboutique.com

tue - sat 11a - 6p sun noon - 5p
online shopping

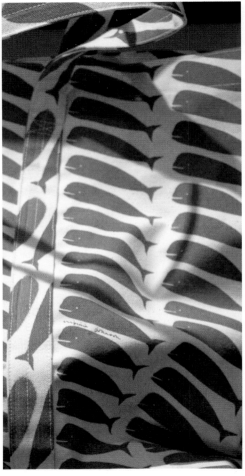

Yes. Please: *demylee sweaters, bo'em plage sandals, virginia johnson scarves & bags, franco ferrari scarves, inhabit sweaters, strenesse, renata jewelry*

When I was shooting Tula, co-owner Laura Westgate was designing her window display with a theme that honored the upcoming summer reading season. She stacked piles of beloved books, hung book pages that she had stitched together, and dressed a mannequin in the perfect seasonal outfit for reading in a hammock. Though it was barely summer, Laura's creative window had me hankering for summer days and the clothing I could wear during them. I could have bought everything in the store at that moment.

andersonville

uptown, lincoln square

eat

e10 big jones
e11 great lake
e12 marigold (off map)
e13 the coffee studio

shop

s10 brimfield
s11 foursided
s12 merz apothecary (off map)
s13 patina
s14 scout
s15 the sweden shop (off map)

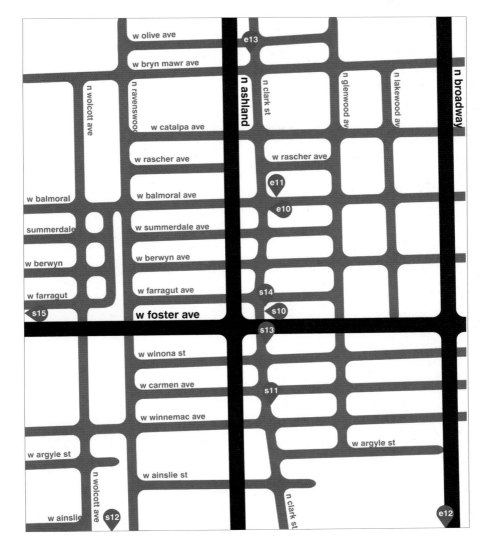

big jones
coastal southern cuisine

5347 North Clark Street
Between Balmoral and Summerdale
(Andersonville) *map E10*
Red Line: Berwyn
773.275.5725
www.bigjoneschicago.com

twitter @bigjones
mon - thu 11a - 9p fri 11a - 10p
sat 9a - 10p sun 9a - 9p
$$-$$$ reservations recommended

Yes, Please: *peter's sazerac, mint julep, lump blue crab cakes, fried green tomatoes, gumbo du jour, carolina pulled pork, fried catfish, mississippi mud pie*

I'm happy that all of the fad food diets—Atkins, South Beach, etc.—are going the way of the dodo, and what people are focusing on more is farm fresh, local, organic ingredients. Frankly, too much worrying about what is and isn't too fattening or carb-rich makes eating lackluster and people grumpy because there isn't much room for eating things like, say, Mississippi mud pie. Or fried anything. What **Big Jones** advocates is a new style of Southern comfort food, which is beautifully prepared and sourced but doesn't have the life sucked out of it on a quest for no fat. I'm going on the **Big Jones** diet.

brimfield

vintage plaids and home accessories

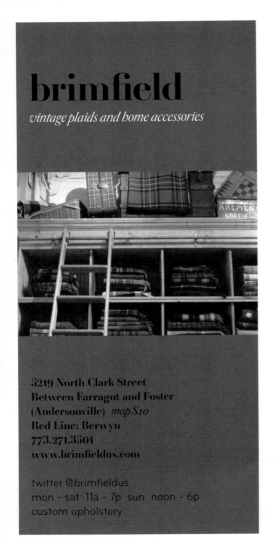

5219 North Clark Street
Between Farragut and Foster
(Andersonville) *map S10*
Red Line: Berwyn
773.271.3504
www.brimfieldus.com

twitter @brimfieldus
mon - sat 11a - 7p sun noon - 6p
custom upholstery

Yes, Please: *plaid blankets, vintage scotch tape tins, pull-down map of the united states, metal buckets, wooden ladders, picnic basket, café brasil pillow, wild fessant*

As I was shooting pictures of Scout for this book, I noticed some activity next door: Another vintage home store, I thought—would it compete with **Scout**? A week later when **Brimfield** opened, I came back to explore. Alas, no competition here, but something much better—a store that is a great complement to **Scout** and a fantastic addition to the neighborhood. **Brimfield** is all about English country chic, and you'll find plaids a-plenty with, of course, brimfield being the most desirable pattern.

foursided

more than just a frame shop

5064 North Clark Street
Corner of Carmen
(Andersonville) *map S11*
See website for other location
Red Line: Argyle
773.506.8300
www.foursided.com

twitter @foursided
see website for hours
custom services

Yes, Please: *vintage flash cards, old maps & prints, wood alphabet blocks; framing: floating frames, special mat design, memory boxes; twosided (foursided's sister store)*

I have a friend, Katie, who is a genius at framing her art in the least expected ways and then hanging it. I, on the other hand, buy art and then let it sit, agonizing over which frame to use and where to hang the piece. Argh. I have found a partial solution to this problem: **Foursided**. Not only are they expert framers here, but take a look around this place. Co-owners Todd Mack and Gino Pinto have a great eye for style—this place is as much a great gift store and gallery as it is a framer. Now I just need to find someone to do the hanging.... Katie, are you available?

great lake

neighborhood pizza joint with
a national rep

1477 West Balmoral Avenue
Corner of Clark (Andersonville) *map E 11*
Red Line: Berwyn
773.334.9270

wed - sat 5p - 9:30p
$$ first come, first served

Yes. Please: *aranciata, pellegrino; pizzas: tomato with*
fresh mozzarella & fresh herbs, cremini mushroom,
pepperoni with arugula & fresh cream

In 1966 journalist Gay Talese wrote a story for Esquire Magazine called "Frank Sinatra Has a Cold." Assigned to write this profile with a quick deadline, Talese wasn't able to actually interview the singer in time because Sinatra had a cold. **Great Lake** is my Frank Sinatra. Between the first time I tried their pies and when I tried to shoot them months later, throngs of people had descended on this perfectly appointed Andersonville B.Y.O. Getting a good shot of the product became a challenge. I'm thinking you don't need a picture of this perfect pie to convince you to come here, though. Just put your trust in me and Frank.

marigold
modern indian

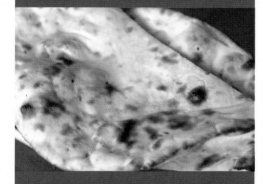

4832 North Broadway Avenue
Between Lawrence and Ainslie
(Uptown) *map E12*
Red Line: Lawrence
773.293.4653
www.marigoldrestaurant.com

twitter @marigold_indian
sun 5 - 9p tue - thu 5:30 - 10p
fri - sat 5:30 - 11p
$$ reservations recommended

Yes, Please: *kingfisher lager, spiked mango lassi, samosas, dahi kabab, corn bhuta & spinach salad, vegetarian thali, tandoori chicken, naan*

My husband has been traveling to India on business recently, and this has made him a know-it-all and absolute expert on the cuisine of this entire vast country. With his newfound expertise, he's turned up his nose at a couple of Indian spots in town. When I brought him to **Marigold**, I thought he would dismiss it as inauthentic because of their modern approach. Wrong-o. As we shoveled hot tikka and fresh naan into our mouths, he gave it his official seal of approval. I hate it when he's right, but was secretly happy he was right about **Marigold**.

merz apothecary

natural personal care + beauty goods

4716 North Lincoln Avenue
Between Lawrence and Leland
(Lincoln Square) *map S12*
See website for other location
Brown Line: Western
773.989.0900
www.merzapothecary.com

twitter @merzapothecary
mon - sat 9a - 6p
online shopping

Yes, Please: *smallflower trading almond milk & saffron soap, grether's pastilles, dr. hauschka, herbacin hand cream, suki skincare, badger stress soother balm, kneipp herbal bath*

Friends, immortality is to be found at Merz Apothecary. Half of the store is dedicated to rejuvenating and improving your health, giving you a good chance at eternal life. The other half is dedicated to keeping your skin youthful and beautiful while you are enjoying this newfound eternal life. Who wants to be sticking around forever without well-nourished, glowing skin? Not I. Beyond all the life-altering and beauty-enhancing potions, aids, and panaceas that abound at **Merz Apothecary**, it's just plain ol' good shopping fun to browse the products here.

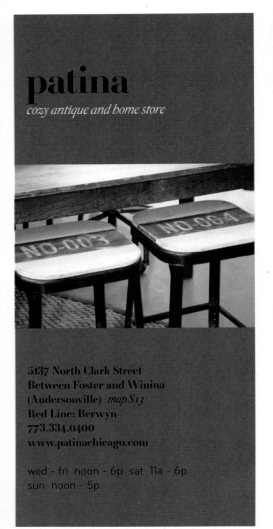

patina
cozy antique and home store

5437 North Clark Street
Between Foster and Winina
(Andersonville) *map S13*
Red Line: Berwyn
773.334.0400
www.patinachicago.com

wed - fri noon - 6p sat 11a - 6p
sun noon - 5p

Yes, Please: *metal cubby, stainless steel kitchen island, university of wisconsin filing cabinet, glass beakers, medicine cabinet, vintage mail sorter*

Some things get so much better with age (wine and antiques) and some get so much worse (electronics and skin around the neck). Alan Shull's store **Patina** is filled with things that are getting better and cooler with every passing day. Filing cabinets can seem humdrum, but not if they are beautifully patina'd filing cabinets from the University of Wisconsin. Same goes for just about everything in this shop, all of which has been carefully chosen by Alan. If only everything aged as well as what can be found here. I'm hoping my neck is listening to me.

scout

scouted vintage pieces

5221 North Clark Street
Between Farragut and Foster
(Andersonville) *map S14*
Red Line: Berwyn
773.275.5700
www.scoutchicago.com

tue - wed 11a - 6p thu - fri noon - 7p
sat 11a - 6p sun noon - 5p

Yes, Please: *aluminum drinking cans, metal crates, wooden crates, mirrors, red cabinet, black lacquered dresser, ben brandt etchings*

Only a handful of shops appeared in all three of the editions of eat.shop chicago, and now the first edition of *rather chicago*. **Scout** is one of them, because whenever I enter Larry Vodak's store, I am happily amazed at how his energy and artfulness are never-ending, how he has the ability to sniff out incredible pieces that almost always sell within days of being on the floor, and how he presents his finds in the most interesting of ways. It's obvious to all that Larry loves what he does, and we the fans love him and **Scout** for all that they bring to Chicago.

the coffee studio

carefully crafted coffee

5628 North Clark Street
Corner of Olive (Andersonvile) *map E13*
Red Line: Bryn Mawr
773.271.7881
www.thecoffeestudio.com

twitter @thecoffeestudio
daily 6:30a - 9p
coffee / tea. light meals. treats
$ first come, first served

Yes, Please: *fresh cup of intelligentsia coffee, cafe au lait, red eye, chai latte, frozen mocha, oatmeal & milk, chemex glass handled brewer & filters*

Though the thought of sitting at a coffee shop working or reading sounds appealing, more often than not the atmosphere is not quite right. I do admit I'm a bit like Goldilocks when it comes to my coffee shop preferences, but I have found one that works for me in all regards: **The Coffee Studio**. This is the brightest and most lovely spot I could imagine for enjoying a morning cup, and its apt use of the word "studio" furthers the point that a bunch of artisans are making the coffee here. Even the porridge (i.e., a yummy little cup of steamed milk oatmeal), is juuuust riiight.

the sweden shop

designs from scandinavia

3304 West Foster Avenue
Between Spaulding and Christiana
(Lincoln Square) *map S15*
Brown Line: Kimball
773.478.0327
www.theswedenshop.com

twitter @swedenshop
mon - sat 10a - 6p sun 10a - 3p

Yes, Please: *lotta jansdotter, royal copenhagen, bodum, anne black, tord boontje, marimekko, orrefors, kosta boda*

I have had such an itch to go to Scandinavia. Copenhagen, Stockholm and Oslo are all at the top of my travel list, and my main motivation is the design sensibilities of this part of the globe. Until I can satisfy my yen by hopping on a flight, I can just hop up north to **The Sweden Shop**. Talk about going to the source. This place carries a collection of all of the rock stars of Scandinavian art and design, from Carl Laarson to Lotta Jansdotter, so you get a taste of both the old and new schools of design. Visiting here is a perfect primer to get me ready for my hopefully-in-the-near-future trip.

roscoe village

logan square, avondale, albany park

eat

shop

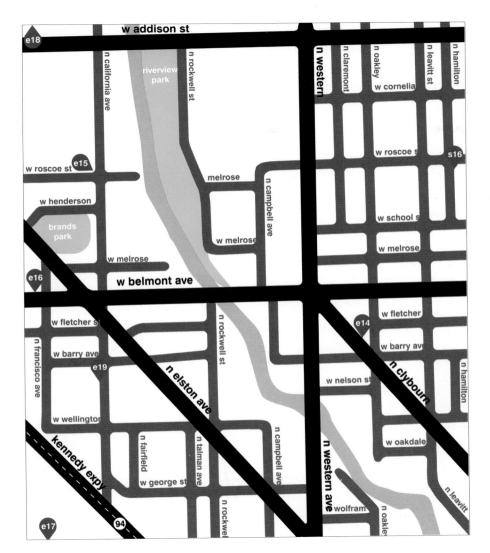

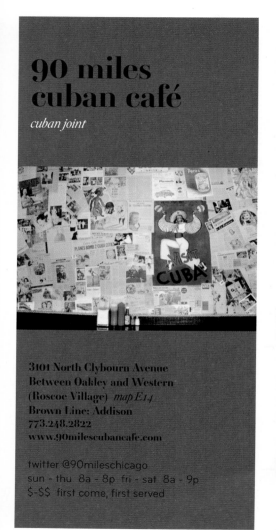

90 miles
cuban café

cuban joint

**3101 North Clybourn Avenue
Between Oakley and Western
(Roscoe Village)** *map E14*
**Brown Line: Addison
773.248.2822
www.90milescubancafe.com**

twitter @90mileschicago
sun - thu 8a - 8p fri - sat 8a - 9p
$-$$ first come, first served

Yes, Please: *malta, iron beer, cubano sandwich,
ropa vieja sandwich, maduros, tostones, yuca rellena,
papa rellena, frijoles negros*

You go 90 miles out from Chicago, you end up, well, somewhere in the middle of Indiana... maybe. You go 90 miles from Miami and you end up in Cuba. But, if you go just a few miles north on Clybourn, you end up at **90 Miles Cuban Café**. Here, you can find Cubano sandwiches, hot plantains, café con leche, and a feeling like you've traveled south and found yourself on the island. Owners Christine and Alberto Gonzalez import the flavors of Cuba to us Chicagoans, which makes me very happy, and very full.

bari zaki
studio

a book-maker's studio

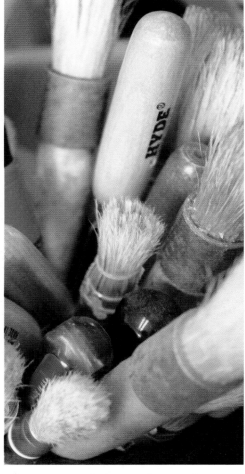

2119 West Roscoe Street
Between Hamilton and Hoyne
(Roscoe Village) *map S16*
Brown Line: Addison
773.294.7766
www.barizaki.com

mon - fri 11a - 7ish sat - sun by appointment
custom orders / design

Yes, Please: *custom books, custom boxes, envelopes made with vintage correspondence & stamps, letterprecious labels, tape escape dots*

As I toured Bari Zaki's immaculately kept studio, I found my mind wandering to the "Spoonful of Sugar" scene from *Mary Poppins.* Bari certainly understands that "in every job that must be done, there is an element of fun." As I perused the custom books and keepsake boxes, I realized that what I really wanted was for Bari to organize my entire life. Unfortunately that isn't a service she offers, so I'll have to be content with some one-of-a-kind note cards or a hand bound book. Whatever you choose here, it will be a lark, a spree, it's very clear to see!

hot doug's

the sausage superstore and encased meat emporium

3324 North California Avenue
Corner of Roscoe (Avondale) *map E15*
CTA Bus: 152 - Addison
773.279.9550
www.hotdougs.com

twitter @hotdougs
mon - sat 10:30a - 4p
$-$$ first come, first served

GAME OF THE WEEK

Brown Ale and Chipotle
BUFFALO SAUSAGE
with Chili-Garlic Mustard and Vintage Farmhouse Cheese
$8.00

Yes, Please: *fresca; hot dogs: the elvis, the paul kelly, the keira knightley, the frankie "five angels" pentangeli, the game of the week; duck fat fries, cheese fries*

Ever since dressing up as "ketchup" in an elaborate handmade costume for Halloween when I was little (my best friend was "mustard"), I have had a special place in my heart for this condiment. I might have even applied it once to a hot dog, a gaffe and no-no I learned upon moving to Chicago. The thing about **Hot Doug's** is that there is no such thing as a no-no—when there's something like a mandarin orange dog or teriyaki chicken sausage dog on the menu, you know rules are being broken. Just don't let anyone see you put ketchup on it.

kuma's corner

rock star burgers

2900 West Belmont Avenue
Corner of Francisco (Avondale) *map E16*
Blue Line: Belmont
773.604.8769
www.kumascorner.com

mon - fri 11:30a - 2a   sat 11:30a - 3a
sun noon - midnight
$$ first come, first served

Yes, Please: *inferno belgian strong ale, surly furious american ipa; burgers: famous kuma burger, black sabbath, judas priest; p.e.i. mussels, fried calamari*

Here's some advice. If you go to **Kuma's Corner**, whatever hour of the day, any day of the week—don't go with an empty stomach. Most of Chicago is also heading to **Kuma's**, and you'll be waiting in line with a bunch of empty, growling stomachs. Now, here's the tricky part: by the time you get a seat and are ready to order one of these rock star burgers, you will need to be famished. These burgers are some serious eating—a strategy is required to get the whole thing down—but there's no doubt this burger sensation is absolutely worth it, and you might not have to eat for a couple of days.

longman & eagle
gastropub, whiskey haven and inn

2657 North Kedzie Avenue
Corner of Schubert
(Logan Square) *map E17*
Blue Line: Logan Square
773.276.7110
www.longmanandeagle.com

twitter @longmanandeagle
mon - fri, sun 9a - 2a sat 9a - 3a
lunch. dinner. brunch
$$-$$$ first come, first served

Yes, Please: *hundreds of whiskeys, english pea agnolotti with wild mushrooms & truffled pea puree & pea shoots, wild boar sloppy joe, beer battered soft shell crabs*

Raise your hand if you have trouble sleeping. It seems every other person I talk to has some degree of sleep disorder. I think a solution could be **Longman & Eagle**. With a couple hundred whiskeys on hand and homey comfort food like sloppy joes, roasted chicken and beef fat fries, this eating and drinking establishment is the first step to getting a good night's sleep. The second step? Feeling so at home here, you decide to book one of the few rooms upstairs. Peace of mind bonus: Chef Jared Wentworth sources locally as often as he can, so even your carbon footprint conscience won't keep you up at night.

the fish guy market

fish monger

4423 North Elston Avenue
Between Montrose and Keeler
(Albany Park) *map E18*
CTA Bus: 53 - Pulaski
773.283.7400
www.fishguy.com

twitter @fishguymarket
mon - sat 10a - 6p
$$ first come, first served

Yes, Please: *colassal king crab legs, sushi grade bluefin tuna, wellfleet oysters, golden trout; lunch: fish tacos, lobster roll, clamwich*

There is much to tell you about The Fish Guy Market and the fish guy himself, Bill Dugan, in such a tiny space—but I'm going to go for it. First, come here for lunch to get insanely yummy fish tacos and lobster rolls. Second, come here for the once-weekly dinner on Friday called Wellfleet, and indulge in a luxurious prix fixe, seafood-laden meal. Third and most importantly, come here to buy fresh, sustainably harvested seafood. So there's many an option to chose from, but if I were you, I would sign on for the whole **Fish Guy** experience: lunch, dinner and some seafood to take home with you.

urban belly

modern dumpling house

3053 North California Avenue
Between Nelson and Barry
(Avondale) *map E19*
Blue Line: California
773.583.0500
www.urbanbellychicago.com

twitter @urbanbelly
tue - sun 11a - 9p
$-$$ first come, first served

Yes. Please: *asian squash & bacon dumplings, pork & cilantro dumplings, organic pea shoots & thai basil rice, short rib & scallion rice*

Pssst. Hey you. Keep your voice down. I've got a secret. One of the best meals to be had in this city these days is at **Urban Belly**. Why am I whispering? Because last time I checked there weren't any crazy lines of foodies snaking out the door that have been spotted at various other places in town of late. So if you can keep this our secret, we will be able to get in here and grab a seat at one of the communal tables without an hour-long wait. Just be careful—don't sit too close to your tablemates, lest they be tempted to snag one of your precious dumplings or a short rib. Heathens.

bucktown

eat

shop

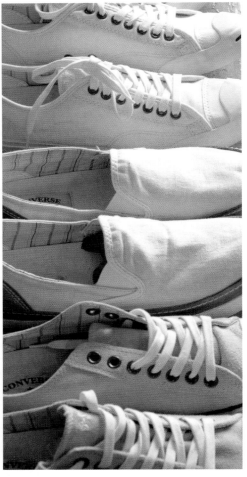

apartment number 9

smart men's shop

1804 North Damen Avenue
Between Churchill and Wabansia
(Bucktown) *map S17*
Blue Line: Damen
773.395.2999
www.apartmentnumber9.com

mon - fri 11a - 7p sat 11a - 6p
sun noon - 5p

Yes, Please: *dries van noten, martin margiela, band of outsiders, paul smith, steven alan, our legacy, trovata, rogues gallery, philip lim, ernest sewn, jack spade*

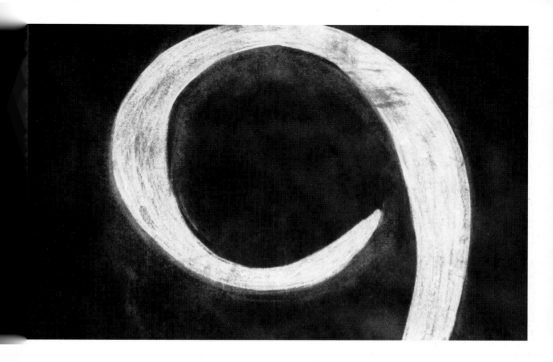

"Apartment Number 9? Your sisters own that store?! Wow." I hear this all the time from new acquaintances, other store owners, total strangers. I've come to realize that my two older sisters have, over the past eight years, developed quite a name for themselves. It's good to get outside confirmation, otherwise I might start to suspect that my conviction that this is the best men's store in the city, maybe the country—maybe the whole darn world— is a little biased. But I love my sisters and I love **Apartment Number 9**.

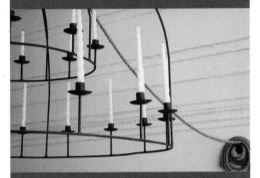

michael
del piero
good design

an interior designer's store

1914 North Damen Avenue
Between Armitage and Cortland
(Bucktown) *map S18*
Blue Line: Damen
773.772.3000
www.michaeldelpiero.com

twitter @delpieromichael
tue - sat 11a - 5p and by appointment
design services

Yes. Please: *baluchi pillows, industrial oval table, antique african berber bench, lucy slivinski lights, mid-century chairs, oversized african vessel*

Nothing is as expected at Michael del Piero Good Design. The first surprise comes from learning that interior designer and shop owner Michael is in fact a female. Another surprise might be that there are as many treasures here from Chicago-based artists as there are from international talents. Michael's ability at creating the unexpected and striking is found at nearly every little glorious corner here, and you may find yourself forever spoiled for anything considered usual or ordinary after visiting this quite extraordinary place.

olivia's
market

*a market with everything you want
and need*

**2014 West Wabansia Avenue
Between Damen and Milwaukee
(Bucktown)** *map E20*
**Blue Line: Damen
773.227.4220
www.oliviasmarket.com**

daily 8a - 9p
grocery
$-$$ first come, first served

Yes, Please: *organic beer, rick's picks pickles, boar's head
meats, fresh produce, carol's cookies, penny candy, just
about anything else you might need*

Once upon a time, there was a lovely couple in Chicago who opened a lovely neighborhood grocery named **Olivia's Market**. It grew to become everyone's favorite place to shop—even little girls and boys who might get a piece of penny candy on the way out if they were especially good. A trip for groceries became enjoyable, no longer a chore. The owners were glad, the shoppers content and everyone lived happily ever after. Author's note: I'm secretly hoping for a sequel, where **Olivia's** opens in my neighborhood. That would be a true fairytale ending.

p.45
long-standing women's boutique

1643 North Damen Avenue
Between North and Wabansia
(Bucktown) *map S19*
Blue Line: Damen
773.862.4523
www.p45.com

mon - sat 11a - 7p   sun noon - 5p
online shopping

Yes, Please: *brochu walker, philip lim 3.1, mason, inhabit, abigail glaum-lathbury, lara miller, eugenia kim, humanoid, designers 4 cure, bensoni, ld tuttle for vpl, lizzie fortunato*

Forgetting all my resolutions to better my self and character, I recently started a list of beauty resolutions. On my list: wear prettier undergarments. Never leave the house without perfume. Drink more water. Tweeze my eyebrows. I am considering adding to this list: shop more often at **p.45**. Everything I've ever bought here instantly makes me feel pretty, and whenever I find myself in this store, co-owners Judy and Tricia inspire me to wear more dresses and get dolled up more often. In general, I take whatever advice these smart and stylish ladies are willing to throw my way.

robin richman

a one-of-a-kind experience

2108 North Damen Avenue
Between Charleston and Dickens
(Bucktown) *map S20*
Blue Line: Damen
773.278.6150
www.robinrichman.com

twitter @robinrichmaninc
mon - sat 11a - 6p sun noon - 5p

Yes, Please: *a détacher, complex geometries, antipast, gary graham, hannoh, rick owens, van bongo, blur leather, johnny farah, antipast, majo, dusica dusica*

I get many requests from store owners across the country wanting their business to be considered for this book and they often ask me what I look for in a store. Here it is: I look for the unusual, the unexpected, a passionate owner, and I need to experience a visceral reaction to the place, i.e., it makes me tingle. What does a place like this look like? **Robin Richman**. This is the one and only store of its kind, a mecca for women who want to dress uniquely. Robin and her store are a grand inspiration for anyone wondering what it means to be an outstanding local business.

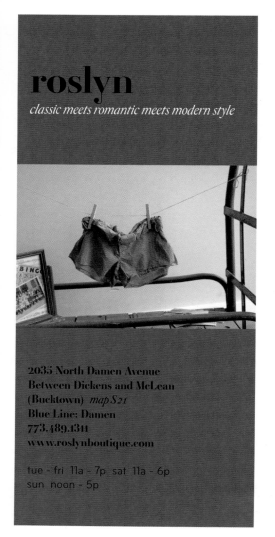

roslyn
classic meets romantic meets modern style

2035 North Damen Avenue
Between Dickens and McLean
(Bucktown) *map S21*
Blue Line: Damen
773.489.1311
www.roslynboutique.com

tue - fri 11a - 7p sat 11a - 6p
sun noon - 5p

Yes. Please: *steven alan, elise bergman, sarah seven, tenoversix, luxury jones, nicholas k, mackage, greylin, mineralogy, plume, jenny sheriff, wendy bassin*

I am in the middle of a style crisis. Somewhere in the last year and a half, I lost my style. I'm pretty upset about it, so if you find it, can you let me know? In the meantime, while I'm searching, I'm thinking of starting over at **Roslyn**. Though this store is all about owner Rosie's style, I'm pretty keen on it, and I'm thinking of stealing it or, rather, swiping my card and paying for it. Rosie's style manages to hit pitch perfect between classic and edgy, dressed-up and dressed-down, romantic and modern—this is just the place to find yourself and your style if it's gone missing, like mine.

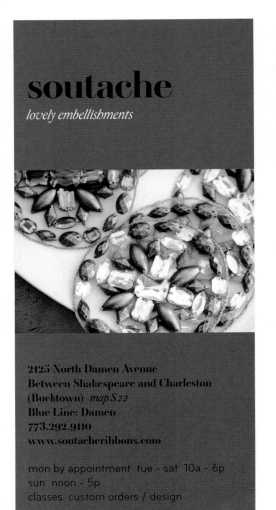

soutache

lovely embellishments

2125 North Damen Avenue
Between Shakespeare and Charleston
(Bucktown) *map S22*
Blue Line: Damen
773.292.9110
www.soutacheribbons.com

mon by appointment tue - sat 10a - 6p
sun noon - 5p
classes. custom orders / design

Yes. Please: *ribbons!, feathers, buttons & more*
buttons, belt buckles, bag handles, embroidering ribbons,
embellishments

I recently bought a sewing machine and now I'm hyper with a million ideas and projects I'd like to embark on. Who is to blame for this excitement? Maili Powell at **Soutache**, for her store is full of things I must have. I'm so amped I'm about to start adding ribbons to my running shoes and embellishing my toolbox. And if you feel like you're clumsy with sewing or crafts yet long for a feathered headband or ribbon-flower brooch, you can either buy one of Maili's own creations or take a class from the pro herself. Just don't blame me when you become addicted to this store.

takashi

french-american meets japanese

1952 North Damen Avenue
Between Armitage and Homer
(Bucktown) *map E21*
Blue Line: Damen
773.772.6170
www.takashichicago.com

twitter @cheftakashi
see website for hours
dinner
\$\$-\$\$\$ reservations recommended

Yes. Please: *blood orange martini, lost in translation cocktail, soy cured scottish salmon, spring roll, sashimi plate, grilled marinated beef short ribs*

You might think that getting a Best New Restaurant of the Year Award might go to a chef's head. Not Takashi's. When I came here to take pictures, a year after *Chicago Magazine* gave him this honor, he was still racing around like a newbie chef—taking reservations, preparing food for the photos, even mixing me a drink—all the while staying jovial as all get out. He said, smiling, "You own your own restaurant, you have to do everything!" No ego at work here. And did I mention the food at **Takashi** is out of this world?

the bluebird

continental wine, beer and food

1749 North Damen Avenue
Between Bloomingdale and Wabansia
(Bucktown) *map E22*
Blue Line: Damen
773.486.2473
www.bluebirdchicago.com

twitter @bluebirdchicago
sun - fri 5p - 2a sat 4p - 3a
dinner
$$ first come, first served

Yes, Please: *le merle saison, dorothy goodbody's stout, helles schlenkerla lagerbier, serrano ham, manchego & egg flatbread, mac & cheese gratin*

Beers can have a lot of different and unusual undertones: raisin, plum, coffee, chocolate. Whatever your beer palate can imagine will be found in one or more of the beers on the list at **The Bluebird**. The menu here is pages long, featuring ales and lagers from all over the world that will satisfy every taste. If you think the beer decision-making process is too tough, then start with some of the fantastic food, where you can't go wrong. And if you discover a beer with a curry undertone, let me know—that sounds interesting.

the whistler

sublime, laid-back cocktail bar

2421 North Milwaukee Avenue
Between Fullerton and Richmond
(Logan Square) *map E23*
Blue Line: California
773.227.3530
www.whistlerchicago.com

twitter @whistlerchicago
see website for hours
bar
$$ first come, first served

Yes, Please: *cocktails: dark & stormy, the old square, blue collar, viking funeral, admiral schley; beer: three floyds, great lakes, bells; whistler records*

I do not like fussy, girly, sweetened, silly-looking cocktails. If I find an umbrella, a small plastic monkey or a neon stir stick in my drink I get surly. What I do love is a precisely executed, creatively crafted cocktail. What do I mean by this? A classy glass (no more martini glasses, please!), nice big ice cubes, carefully chosen spirits, and house-made syrups and infusions. Hence my fondness for **The Whistler**. The cocktails are so good here (and never silly), and the place so understatedly cool, you might find an unexpected line out the door of its unexpected location.

wicker park

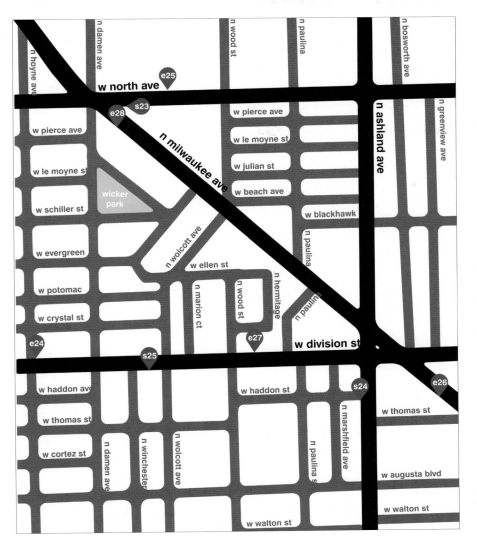

asrai garden
an exquisite floral store

1935 West North Avenue
Between Damen and Wood
(Wicker Park) *map S23*
Blue Line: Damen
773.782.0680
www.asraigarden.com

twitter @asraigarden
mon - sat 10a - 7p sun noon - 4p
deliveries. weddings. events

Yes. Please: *flowers!!, herbes de cèment, john derian, laura zindel, patch nyc, tamar mogendorff, santa maria novella, caskata, form and pheromone by christopher marley*

I recently decided that some of the best gifts are ones that disappear quickly: wine, homemade baked goods and flowers. These are all items that take up no permanent space and add no extra clutter. That's why I like to give (and even better, receive) arrangements from **Asrai Garden**. Though there is one small problem. I never want **Asrai**'s flowers to go away. Someone once gave me a sweet little bouquet from here that I adored. It sat in my room for weeks past its prime because I was so sad to part with it. The only solution is to treat yourself and your friends at **Asrai** regularly.

crust

organic wood-oven pizza

2056 West Division Street
Corner of Hoyne (Wicker Park) *map E24*
Blue Line: Damen
773.235.5511
www.crustorganic.com

twitter @crusteatreal
sun - thu 11:30a - 10p
fri - sat 11:30a - midnight
$$ first come, first served

Yes, Please: *three floyds gumballhead ale, two brothers cane & ebel rye beer, arugula salad, caesar salad; wood-oven pizzas: shroom, wild herb & cheese, pepperonata*

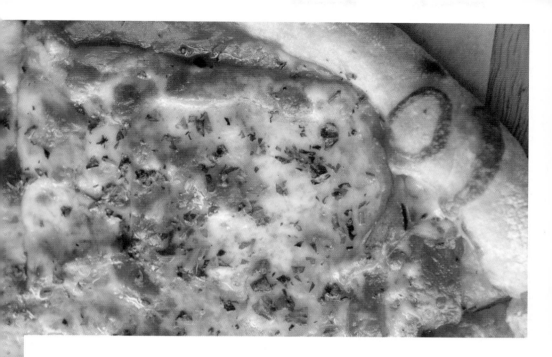

There are warmer, sunnier places to live in the world than Chicago. But if there were sun around all the time, we wouldn't have our annual "coming out" party, which happens during the first week of warm weather, and the whole darn city comes out of hiding. It does get a bit dodgy though, as people go cuckoo securing places to eat outdoors. I'll save you the hunt for where to go for al fresco dining: **Crust**. Out on the back patio, guzzling organic beers and wood-oven pizzas, Chicagoans and visitors alike will get what makes a few million people stick around here through the godforsaken winters.

kokorokoko

fashions from the '80s, '90s and '00s

**1112 North Ashland Avenue
Between Division and Augusta
(Wicker Park)** *map S24*
**Blue Line: Division
773.252.6996
www.koko-rokoko.blogspot.com**

twitter @kokorokoko
mon – sat noon – 8p sun noon – 6p

Yes, Please: *vintage: vests, keds, polka dots, neon, waist packs, shoulder pads, acid-wash denim, bomber jackets, banana cut jeans, scrunchies*

When I first met co-owner Sasha Hodges at Kokorokoko she was wearing crazily patterned, somehow amazingly flattering, shiny spandex leggings. If there's anybody out there who knows how to wear things like scrunchies and acid wash, it's Sasha—she's the guru of polka dots, shoulder pads, Keds, fanny packs, and neon. No late 20th century trends have been overlooked. These are the styles of my youth, so I'm rejoicing that they are experiencing a renaissance. Now, if only I hadn't gotten rid of my parachute pants. Hopefully **Kokorokoko** will have some.

lillie's q

authentic and cool bbq

1856 West North Avenue
Corner of Wolcott (Wicker Park) *map E25*
Blue Line: Damen
773.772.5500
www.lilliesq.com

twitter @lilliesqchicago
sun - wed 11a - 10p thu - sat 11a - 11p
lunch. dinner
$$ first come, first served

Yes, Please: *lillie's q brew, fried pickles, sweet potato fries, boiled peanuts, pulled pork sandwich, brunswick stew, low country boil, taste of lq, banana pudding, shortcake*

I was surprised to discover that some of the best barbeque around is happening just off the chronic traffic jam of North and Damen in Bucktown. Though the intersection is busy, the meat smoking at **Lillie's Q** is slow and low. Charlie Mckenna is using family recipes from South Carolina to create his menu, which is full of my top southern favorites: boiled peanuts, sweet tea, banana pudding, and my, oh, my, the pulled pork! The only dilemma is which barbeque sauce to choose, but luckily you don't have to, as each table is armed with an array of them all. If there were ever a place worth fighting through bumper-to-bumper traffic to get to, it's **Lillie's Q**.

lovely
a bake shop and café

4130 North Milwaukee Avenue
Between Augusta and Division
(Wicker Park) *map E26*
Blue Line: Division
773.572.4766
www.lovelybakeshop.com

mon - fri 7a - 5p sat 9a - 5p sun 9a - 4p
$-$$ first come, first served

Yes, Please: *reed's ginger brew, goose island root beer, pb & j sandwich, blueberry muffin, banana pecan muffin, raspberry linzer coffee cake*

On any given day, I swing between realism and pessimism (these days that's not a big swing). Except when I've been to **Lovely**, where my perspective changes to rosy, sweet optimism, and the world seems, well. . . lovely. I think this is the effect in general of being around baked goods, though this whole place gives off a sort of old timey "gee shucks, ain't life grand?" vibe that makes you more than happy to forget your woes. So next time you're stuck in doom mood, just come to **Lovely** to improve your perspective with a good dose of butter, sugar and eggs.

mana food bar

amazing vegetarian food

4742 West Division Street
Between Wood and Paulina
(Wicker Park) *map E27*
Blue Line: Division
773.342.4742
www.manafoodbar.com

sun - thu 4 - 10p fri 4 - 11p
sat noon - 11p
$-$$ first come, first served

Yes. Please: *chai plum & nigori sake, cucumber sakerita;*
chickpeas, red quinoa, thai pineapple salad; bi bim bop,
mana slider, sweet potato pancake

Mana Food Bar embodies the very best of what vegetarianism can be. You'll find no tofurkey here, nor will you find veggie ribs or fake steak. **Mana** shows off vegetables as vegetables, with seductive dishes like mushroom sliders and Thai pineapple salad. These are all foods that might make you wonder why you ever threw a fit about eating your veggies when you were little (or last week, for that matter). To all the hearty meat eaters out there (Hello, Chicago!), come here and just tell me that you're lacking for anything. I dare you.

penelope's

fun clothes for guys and gals

1913 West Division Street
Between Wolcott and Damen
(Wicker Park) *map S25*
Blue Line: Division
773.395.2351
www.shoppenelopes.com

twitter @shoppenelopes
mon - sat 11a - 7p sun noon - 6p
online shopping

Yes, Please: *apc, something else, dusen dusen, nombre, sessun, dolce vita, sebago, fidelity by gerald & stewart, pendleton portland, brooklyn tailors, j.d. fisk, spiewak*

Recently I was on an overseas flight with a woman wearing a fitted, short dress and stilettos. A few rows back, a girl wore sweats and sneakers. I like to think I fall somewhere in the middle of these two dressing styles (and hopefully not close to either). Finding chic, comfortable travel wear has always been a challenge—but no longer. **Penelope's** stocks the perfect fun, kicky outfits for travel of any sort—by plane, train, car, or foot. Though if you've ever sported stilettos on a transatlantic flight before, this store might not be for you.

taxim

greek cuisine

1558 North Milwaukee Avenue
Between North and Honore
(Wicker Park) *map E28*
Blue Line: Damen
773.252.1558
www.taximchicago.com

see website for hours
$$-$$$ reservations recommended

Yes. Please: *06 domaine skouras viognier, 05 domain
karydas xinomavro, piperies, faki, melitzanosalata,
rampopita, arnaki me kapnisto pligouri, duck gyro*

When I think about where to eat, I often think about it in seasonal terms. There are certain spots I head to when it's frigid outside so I can warm up with hearty food—I put Belgian, German and French places in this category. Then there's the other side of the weather report for eating, places where the food is refreshing and light—think sushi. What do I feel like in any weather? **Taxim**. This stellar Greek restaurant works for me year round, with food that seems to work with any season.

west town

ukrainian village, humboldt park,
noble square

eat

e29 black dog gelato
e30 chickpea
e31 hoosier mama pie
e32 old oak tap
e33 rootstock (off map)
e34 ruxbin

shop

s26 dovetail
s27 post 27
s28 sprout home
s29 state street salvage
s30 urban remains
s31 uusi (off map)

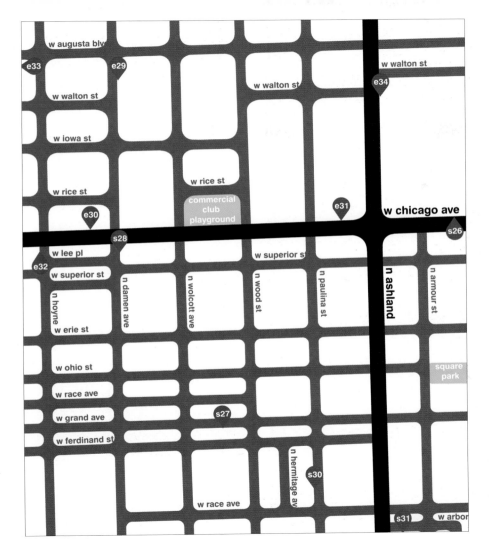

black dog gelato

artisanal gelato

859 North Damen Avenue
Corner of Iowa
(Ukrainian Village) *map E29*
Green/Pink Lines: Ashland
Blue Line: Damen
773.235.3116
www.blackdogchicago.com

mon 5 – 11p sun, tue - thu noon - 11p
fri - sat noon - midnight
treats
$ first come, first served

Yes, Please: *gelato: 3 floyds, strawberry balsamic, malted vanilla, blood orange sorbet, lemon ginger, salted peanut, goat cheese; whiskey gelato bar*

When you spend a few days in Italy, it feels like a frantic rush to consume as much gelato as you can get your hands on. When I spent a year abroad in Rome, I was more leisurely about my gelato consumption, sampling the stuff when I was so inclined. Therefore you'd think that because Chicago is my hometown, I would feel that same leisure with **Black Dog Gelato**. Not so. When I find myself here I feel frenzied, like I must consume every flavor on the menu as though it's my last day on earth. My greatest fear is that I might miss one of Jessica Oloroso's constantly changing creations. Thank goodness for their no-limits rule on tasting.

chickpea

palestinian café

2018 West Chicago Avenue
Between Damen and Hoyne
(Ukrainian Village) *map E30*
Blue Line: Division
773.384.9930
www.chickpeaonthego.com

daily 11a – 10p
$-$$ cash only, first come, first served

Yes, Please: *vinto cream soda, apple/carrot juice, arabian tea, hummus, falafel sandwich, fasoolya, mujaddara, malfoof, mama's choice, baklava*

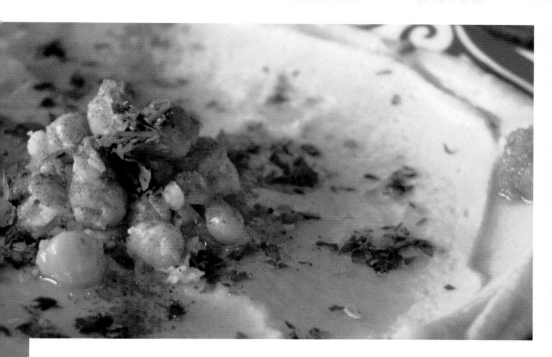

Ah, the glorious chickpea. Mashed, puréed, sautéed, crisped, baked, or fried, I will take it any way it is served, but most of all, I will take it at its namesake restaurant, **Chickpea**. This family business is run by Palestinian natives, with mom in the kitchen making home-cooked food the way her sons love it. Lucky for all of us that the sons are willing to share their mom's cooking talents. Just be sure to clean your plate, or you might get a talking to from the lady in charge. No worries—this is the kind of place you won't want to leave a single morsel behind.

dovetail

vintage for men, women and home

1452 West Chicago Avenue
Between Greenview and Bishop
(Ukrainian Village) *map S26*
CTA Bus: 66 - Chicago
312.243.3100
www.dovetailchicago.com

twitter @dovetailchicago
wed - fri 1 - 8p sat 11a - 6p sun 11a - 5p

Yes, Please: *vintage: gold metallic clutch, vintage cigarette case, '40s black dress, '70s blue pleather raincoat, renoir copper belt, satin mink hat*

I recently decided to try to stop multitasking. Then I came to **Dovetail**, where Jennifer Clower and Julie Ghatan take this sometimes dubious skill to a brilliant new level. They both maintain other jobs (Jennifer is co-owner of **Lustre Skin Boutique**), and yet somehow they dug out the time and creative energy to open this adorable shop filled with extremely desirable vintage pieces for guys and gals. They even have the occasional art opening and party at the store. How do they find the time? They are multitasking prodigies, I decided. Maybe doing two things at once really is the answer.

hoosier mama
pie company
homemade pie

1618 1/2 West Chicago Avenue
Between Ashland and Marshfield
(Ukrainian Village) *map E31*
Blue Line: Division
312.243.4846
www.hoosiermamapie.com

twitter @hmpc
tue - thu 8a - 7p fri 8a - 9p
sat 9a - 5p sun 10a - 4p
$-$$ first come, first served

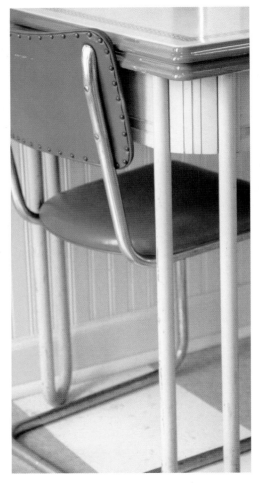

Yes, Please: *diner coffee; pies: classic apple, strawberry rhubarb, banana cream, lemon meringue, maple pecan, chocolate chess, friday night flights*

Cakes come and go. Cupcakes are so five years ago (though I would never turn one down). But pie... pie is forever. It's classic and dependable, yesterday and tomorrow—oh, and it's very of the moment. How do I know? Well, for one, when Paula Haney opened her little pie shop, it took me days before I could get my hands on a slice—I kept showing up to a sold-out shop. Sad. When I finally did get to dig into a fresh slice, all I could think about was coming back as soon as I could for another sweet, homey, comforting piece of pie. So, **Hoosier Mama**? Pie's your mama.

old oak tap

good beer and good food

2109 West Chicago Avenue
Between Hoyne and Leavitt
(Ukrainian Village) *map E32*
CTA Bus: 66 - Chicago
773.772.0406
www.theoldoaktap.com

twitter @oldoaktap
mon 5p - 2a tue - fri 11a - 2a
sat 10a - 3a sun 10a - 2a
$-$$ first come, first served

Yes, Please: *ayinger brau-weisse, magic hat #9,*
pork sampler, homemade soft pretzels, baja style
fish tacos, fat boy pie, deep fried banana stuffed twinkie

Chicago is a beer town. It always has been. But these days a new sort of beer obsession has evolved—the hops gang has developed a hankering for really good, locally brewed beers and unusual varieties that come from faraway lands. **Old Oak Tap** is the ideal place to check out this new scene, as the beer menu is super diverse and it's matched up with some downright great bar food. A pork sampler, you say? Why, yes please. And for you stick-in-the-mud types—and you know who you are—there's an old favorites beer list here just for you, too.

post 27

*an urban destination for mid-century
modern furniture and home goods*

**4819 West Grand Avenue
Between Damen and Wood
(West Town)** *map S27*
**Pink / Green Lines: Ashland - Lake
312.829.6122
www.post27store.com**

tue - fri 11a - 7p sat - sun 11a - 6p

Yes, Please: *bladon connor furniture, unison porter sheets,
vintage globes, kindling faceted rocks, vintage trays &
glassware, green sawn bench, white door credenza*

In my travels, I often find myself in stores where three quarters of the store is well put together and merchandised, and a quarter of the store—usually in the back—is a dark and neglected, dusty little area that holds unwanted things. This is not the story at **Post 27**. Every square inch of this store is beautiful and charming. Each vintage and modern product draws you in with personal vignettes and stories and little scenes. Store owners, take a lesson from **Post 27**: go forth and revive that ignored back corner of your store that is getting the sorry shaft.

rootstock

locally focused wine & beer bar

954 North California Avenue
Corner of Augusta
(Humboldt Park) *map E33*
773.292.1616
www.rootstockbar.com

twitter @rootstockbar
mon - sat 5p - 2a sun 11a - 4p
dinner. brunch
$$-$$$ first come, first served

Yes, Please: *three floyds blackheart ipa, meinklang ancient grains ale, gunthorp farm chicken wings, whitefish brandade, black earth organic burger*

I have been compared to Goldilocks more than once in my life, for my never-ending choosiness as to, well, everything. When it comes to restaurants, my bouts of hypersensitivity only increase. One place is too big; one too loud; another too stuffy; one too fancy. It takes a lot of sitting in dining chairs for me to find the one that fits just right. At **Roostock** I found my match: a laid-back place filled with happy imbibers drinking beer and wine from small-scale producers and eating locally grown food, simply and beautifully prepared. It's the perfect middle ground of casual deliciousness—not too big, not too small. Each mismatched chair at **Rootstock** is just right.

ruxbin

american bistro with french and asian flavors

851 North Ashland Avenue
Corner of Pearson
(Noble Square) *map E34*
Blue Line: Division
312.624.8509
www.ruxbinchicago.com

twitter @ruxbinchicago
tue - sat 5:30 - 10p sun 5:30 - 9p
dinner, byob
$$-$$$ first come, first served

Yes, Please: *housemade dry soda; cured salmon with kalamata olive puree, orange, daikon & golden beets; berry shortcake with balsamic & crème chantilly*

I've always thought chefs were like painters—temperaments included. Edward Kim reminds me of Marc Chagall in his ability to throw together so many things onto one canvas, tell a story, and never risk muddling the elements. Just as you're drawn into a Chagall painting with the many colors and storylines, I was drawn into Edward's unique and surprising flavors. The food isn't the only art on display at **Ruxbin**—take a look at the decoupage ceiling and the creatively crafted interior, and you'll realize that this trio can magically transform any blank slate into a work of art.

sprout home
a garden and home shop

745 North Damen Avenue
Between Chicago and Superior
(Ukrainian Village) *map S28*
CTA Bus: 66 - Chicago
312.226.5950
www.sprouthome.com

twitter @sprout_home
mon - fri 9a - 8p sat - sun 9a - 7p
indoor plant design services

Yes, Please: *binth pillows, sunprint kits, tillandsias, stylish bird house, recycled metal wire bird cage, copenhagen terrarium, bloom in bag*

I've recently been spending a lot of time in Portland, Oregon, where my parents live. They're both gardeners, so I am completely spoiled by their lush, green garden. When I return to my concrete and glass home in Chicago, I'm reminded that I need some green, and therefore I need **Sprout Home**. It helps my cravings to simply wander through the plants here, and I'm pretty sure that a terrarium filled with succulents will fit right in at my mod condo yet will still survive the dry, harsh winter. Thank goodness for the green thumbs at **Sprout Home**.

state street salvage

hand-crafted, salvaged furniture

2248 West Grand Avenue
Between Oakley and Leavitt
(West Town) *map S29*
Green/Pink Lines: Ashland
630.863.9941
www.statestreetsalvage.com

thu - sat 11a - 7p sun 11a - 6p

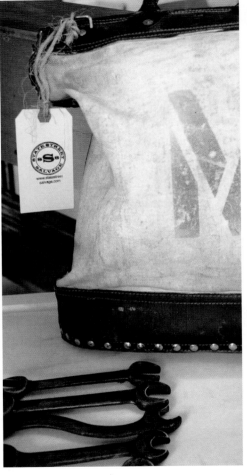

Yes, Please: *baker's rack, machine coil lamp, warehouse banana bin, highway torch lamp, factory work bench, blueprint cabinet*

There are dumpster divers. And roadside shoppers. And urban anthropologists who dig through teardown building sites. Owners Kevin Hanley and Steve Peterson may have been all of the above at some point or another, but first and foremost they are artists and craftsmen, salvaging cast-off wares and reworking them into one-of-a-kind handmade works of art. **State Street Salvage** is their gallery-shop-studio, where these gorgeous pieces are created, making these guys the ultimate recyclers. It's hard to imagine this collection of beauties with a past ever being cast aside again.

urban remains

antique architectural artifacts

4850 West Grand Avenue
Between Wood and Wolcott
(Ukrainian Village) *map S30*
Pink/Green Lines: Ashland - Lake
312.492.6254
www.urbanremainschicago.com

twitter @urbanremains
mon - fri 11a - 6p sat - sun 11a - 5p
online shopping

Yes, Please: *'20s light fixtures, exterior building elements, antique mantles, vintage signs, millwork, period hardware, leaded glass windows*

Do you sometimes wonder what will remain of this city in a hundred years? Will it be like *Wall-E*, where our garbage will have overtaken everything and we'll have to leave earth to live on a spaceship? I hope not. I'm hoping that, instead, there will be amazing places like **Urban Remains**, that people can buy and repurpose the greatest hits of architecture, technology, furniture, signage, lighting, and miscellany. Recycling and re-using via a cool shop like **Urban Remains** seems a much better way to manage our throw-aways than letting it all pile up, doesn't it?

uusi

timeless, beautiful objects

321 North Justine Street
Between Carroll and Fulton
(Ukrainian Village) *map S31*
773.576.8220
http://uusi.us

by appointment only
online shopping

Yes, Please: *moderne farm animals, storage boxes, cutting & serving boards, puukko knife holder, one-of-a-kind wooden fishing lures*

Peter and Linnea, the creative team behind Uusi, don't have a store, and it's a good thing they don't, because no one would ever leave. I have found myself on more than one occasion lingering a little too long during a visit to their studio, where they make beautiful hand crafted objects. To say I was stretching my welcome is an understatement. Though the studio is not open to the public, the good news is that you can shop online, allowing you to instill some of **Uusi's** Danish style and sensibility into your own home. Watch out, though; if you buy too many of these delightful objects to put on display, your guests may never want to leave either.

river west

west loop

eat

shop

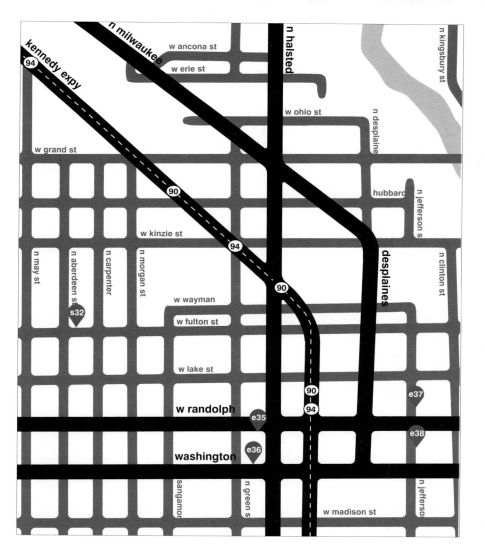

girl & the goat

new american, cool american

809 West Randolph Street
Between Halsted and Green
(West Loop) *map E35*
Green Line: Clinton - Green
312.492.6262
www.girlandthegoat.com

sun - thu 4:30 - 11p
fri - sat 4:30 - midnight
dinner
$$-$$$ reservations accepted

Yes, Please: *three floyds alpha king, squash blossom rangoon, fried soft-shell crab, wood-oven roasted pigface, goat chorizo flat bread*

We like to say that these books seek out the off-the-beaten path places in town. Needless to say, **Girl & the Goat**'s path is so well beaten, it needs repaving. So why add to the chorus of praise? Because sometimes places are just that good. And because our admiration and affection for chef/owner Stephanie Izard goes back to her pre-reality show fame days at her first restaurant **Scylla**, and we've been waiting for her next endeavor ever since. So be forewarned: You will have to share **Girl & the Goat** with many others, it won't just be your secret, but I guarantee this won't make your time at **G & G** any less divine.

morlen sinoway atelier

inspired interiors and accessories

1052 West Fulton Market
Corner of Aberdeen
(West Loop) *map S32*
Green/Pink Lines: Clinton
312.432.0100
www.morlensinoway.com

twitter @sinowayatelier
mon - fri 9:30a - 5p sat 11:30a -5p
and by appointment
custom orders. design services. registries

Yes, Please: *custom furniture, navajo beaded kitchen tools, raumgestalt supersize oak board, rina menardi quadro cups, kühn keramik plates, hml berlin napkin rings*

A handwritten note on a chalkboard in Morlen Sinoway struck me: Dress your home the way you dress yourself. I'm pretty sure that this bit of advice—and the wares in this hugely creative store—have solved just about any home decorating conundrum I might run into with two simple solutions: 1. Reference your own personal style and translate that to your own home, and 2. Shop at **Morlen Sinoway** to add interest, color, personality, and excitement to all of your spaces. Thank you, Morlen, for inspiring and simplifying.

perman wine selections

where wine resolutions come true

**802 West Washington Boulevard
Between Halsted and Green
(West Loop)** *map E36*
**Pink Line: Clinton - Green
312.666.4447
www.permanwine.com**

twitter @permanwine
tue - fri noon - 8p sat 11a - 7p
$$$ first come, first served

Yes, Please: *08 ardilla tempranillo, 08 domaine de la pépière "cuvée granit," 07 vietti barbera d'asti "tre vigne," 06 carm vinho tinto douro*

Some people make New Year's resolutions to lose weight, exercise more, drink less. Not Craig Perman. He made a resolution to drink a glass of champagne every day, all year long. He made it six months or so and then got a bit bubbly-ed out. When some people give up, they walk away from their resolutions completely. In Craig's case—it's not like he could or would lose interest in the grape—he's a veritable encyclopedia of wine knowledge. I suggest your next resolution—and one you should stick to—is to visit **Perman Wine Collection** for a bit of vino knowledge.

province

modern american with spanish and
south american influences

461 North Jefferson Street
Between Randolph and Lake
(West Loop) *map E37*
Green/Pink Lines: Clinton
312.669.9900
www.provincerestaurant.com

twitter @provincechicago
mon – thu 11:30a – 10:30p
fri 11:30a – 11:30p sat 5 – 11:30p
$$-$$$ reservations recommended

Yes, Please: *yellow moon cocktail, house smoked sable ceviche, slow roasted gunthorp farms pork ropa vieja, chimichurri rubbed flatiron steak, chocolate three ways*

Living a green lifestyle in the big city can be challenging, though there are some helpful things that come with the territory: using public transit, walking, living in small apartments that are like 1/2 of a carbon footprint. Composting from a high-rise is doable but harder. Another way to be eco-friendly in Chicago? Eat at **Province**. Housed in a LEED-certified city building (check), a few paces from the El (double check), a chef that is serving gorgeous food that covers all the important eco bases: locally sourced, organic and seasonal. See, this eco thing is not that hard after all.

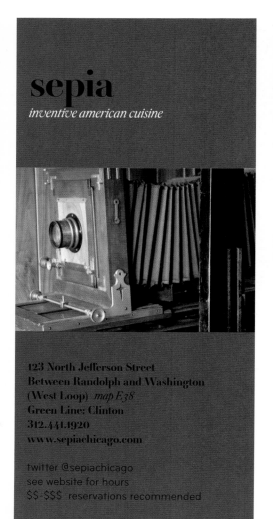

sepia

inventive american cuisine

123 North Jefferson Street
Between Randolph and Washington
(West Loop) *map E38*
Green Line: Clinton
312.441.1920
www.sepiachicago.com

twitter @sepiachicago
see website for hours
$$-$$$ reservations recommended

Yes, Please: *cognac et framboise cocktail, jalisco kiss cocktail, lamb shoulder, caramelized onions & olives, charred baby octopus, duck fat fried potatoes*

I like to plan. I've never met a reservation, calendar or list I didn't like. On occasion, though, I like to break free from my mental tidiness and embrace a *que sera, sera* attitude. On this rare occasion, I like to pop into **Sepia**, grab a seat at the bar, and kick back with a gorgeous cocktail and something mouth-watering from the menu. Sure I could make a reservation, which would be the smart thing to do to ensure a table here, but something about **Sepia** inspires me to be a bit more daring. I suggest, though, that you put **Sepia** on your list.

pilsen
south loop

eat

shop

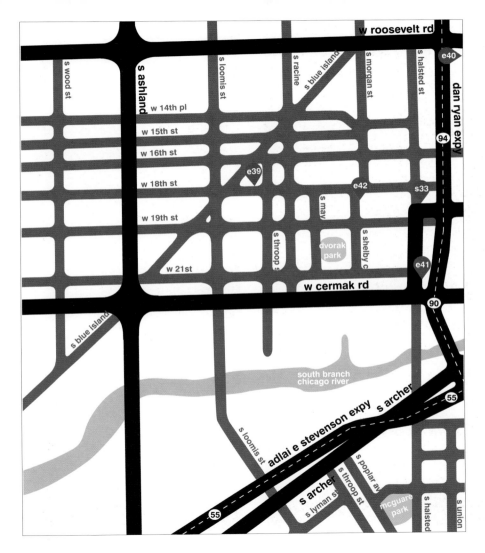

birrieria reyes de ocotlán

la major birria de todo el mundo

1322 West 18th Street
Between Ada and Throop
(Pilsen) *map E39*
Pink Line: 18th
312.733.2643

mon - fri 9a - 8p sat - sun 7a - 8p
$ cash only. first come, first served

Yes. Please: *horchata, piña jamaica, birria de res (beef) taco, birria de chivo (goat) taco, lengua (tongue) taco, goat stew, mexican rice, tortillas*

You might find yourself on 18th street in Pilsen, knowing that somewhere in this neighborhood there is a darn good taco just waiting for you. There are, in fact, many delicious tacos in this 'hood and a constant debate as to which taco is tops. There isn't much of a debate, however, as to which place earns the title Best Goat Taco—that honor goes to **Birrieria Reyes de Ocotlán**. From the moment you see the goat painted on the window, you know what to order. Pair the goat taco with some goat stew and you've got yourself one hearty lunch.

deliciously vintage

vintage for women

1747 South Halsted Street
Between 17th and 18th (Pilsen) *map S33*
Orange Line: Halsted
312.733.0407
www.dvchicago.com

twitter @delishchicago
tue - sat noon - 7p sun by appointment
online shopping

Yes, Please: *vintage: ralph lauren, fendi, christian dior, halston, clutches, $5 rack; dv signature tee*

While raving recently about Pilsen, I've heard a few grumbles from people about it being too far to visit. Come on! Too far is Detroit... Pilsen and **Deliciously Vintage** are just a couple of miles away from wherever you are in Chicago. Think about it: all of the serious legwork is being done here by co-owners Law and Siobhan, as they are constantly on the prowl to fill their vintage store with primo finds. This means you can skip the trips to suburban estate sales and know they are doing the traveling for you. I bet you are now thinking that **Deliciously Vintage** is just a short jaunt away.

little branch cafe

a sweet little cafe

1251 South Prairie Avenue
Corner of 13th (South Loop) *map E40*
Red Line: Roosevelt
312.360.0101
www.littlebranchcafe.com

twitter @thelittlebranch
mon - tue 7a - 4p wed - fri 7a - 10p
sat 8a - 6p sun 8a - 4p
$$ first come, first served

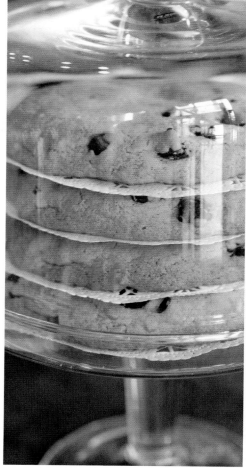

Yes. Please: *fruit smoothies, espresso, yogurt parfait, french toast, breakfast frittata sandwich, nutella banana sandwich, fig jam prosciutto sandwich*

Remember the children's book that tells the story of the little baby bird who falls from his nest, loses his mother, then sets out on a quest for home, and memorably asks a steam shovel, "Are you my mother?" I feel a little like this lost bird while searching for a good, homey lunch in Chicago. After several places that didn't fit the bill, I found my home at **Little Branch**. Tucked a ways off the beaten path, it might take a bit of looking for, but once you find yourself in this sweet little spot, you'll feel as happy as that baby bird who found both his home and his mother.

nightwood
modern heartland cooking

2119 South Halsted Street
Between 21st and Cermak (Pilsen) *map E 41*
Red Line: Cermak
312.526.3385
www.nightwoodrestaurant.com

twitter @nightwoodpilsen
mon – sat 5:30 – 11p
brunch sun 9a – 2:30p
$$–$$$ first come, first served

Yes, Please: *06 alexander valley vineyards cabernet franc, mixed lettuces with croutons, olive oil & vinegar; chilled asparagus soup; raviolo with egg yolk, brown butter & sage*

I often fantasize about writing a national version of this book, which would be an edited selection of my top picks across the country. First on the list from Chicago? **Nightwood**. Once I learned that **Lula Cafe's** owners were opening a new place, I waited anxiously for what seemed like forever. I was sooo excited I worried that the actual moment might be a disappointment. I'm happy to say that **Nightwood** has not brought me an ounce of disappointment—my only issue is that I just can't seem to get back here often enough.

simone's

a cool neighborhood place

960 West 18th Street
Corner of Morgan (Pilsen) *map E42*
Orange Line: Halsted
312.666.8601
www.simonesbar.com

twitter @simonesbar
daily 11:30a - 2a
$$ first come, first served

Yes, Please: *metropolitan flywheel lager, bear republic racer, housemade tomato soup, tempura vegetables, monte cristo sandwich*

What does it mean to you when you hear somebody say a restaurant is a "great neighborhood place"? My translation: the restaurant is somewhat mediocre—good enough for those that are close by, but not good enough to go out of your way to visit. Then there's **Simone's**. Guess what? It's a great neighborhood place. But let me be clear. I'm not saying it's good just for Pilsen; it's good enough to get in your car in Andersonville and come over here. Maybe you'll love it so much here, you'll make **Simone's** your favorite place of the 'hood known as Chicago.

south side

bridgeport

eat

shop

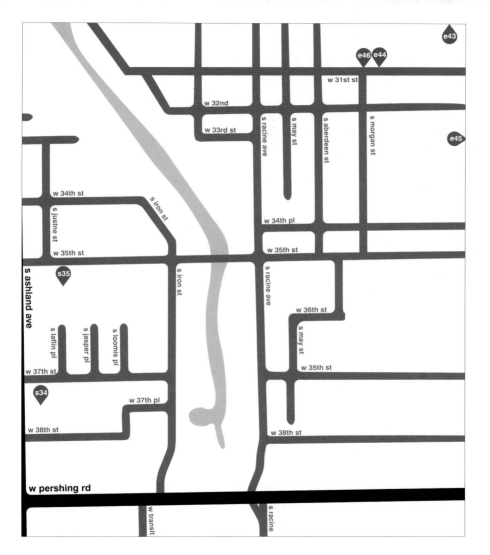

great american cheese collection

a warehouse of great cheese

4727 South Talman Street
Between 47th and 48th
(South Side) *map E43*
Orange Line: Western
773.779.5055
www.greatamericancheese.com

sat 10a - 1p
$-$$ first come, first served

Yes, Please: *fig salumi; cheese: the mayor of nye beach, sunset bay, pennsylvania noble mature, organic caraway gouda, aged swiss emmentaler, organic aged cheddar "fait gras"*

I know what I'll be doing with my Saturdays from now on. I'll be heading down to the **Great American Cheese Collection** warehouse. Giles Schnierle used to sell his cheese solely to a group of the city's best restaurants, but now he's been kind enough to also offer his cheeses to all of us lay folk, working out of a warehouse on the South Side, every Saturday. Here are some tips: First, whatever he's offering for sample, you try. Second, you might as well clear your Saturday mornings until the end of time, because one trip in and you'll want to become a regular.

maria's pack- aged goods & community bar

craft beers, artisanal cocktails

**960 West 31st Street
Corner of Morgan
(Bridgeport)** *map E44*
**CTA Bus: 62
773.890.0588
www.community-bar.com**

see website for hours
liquor store. bar
$ first come, first served

Yes. Please: *more than 370 craft beers & ales,
the hornswagglers high tea, the 11th ward old fashioned,
hardscrabble sazerac*

"No way," said Ed Marszewski when I told him I was putting Maria's Packaged Goods & Community Bar in the book, *"You're going to have a Bridgeport map in the book?!"* Yes, Ed, **Maria's** and next door neighbor **Pleasant House Bakery** have put Bridgeport on the map in a serious way for anyone who wasn't already down here eating at **Nana**. Though we'll give you some help in finding this spot with a map, you have to discover the hidden bar on your own (hint: all is not as it appears in this little beer, wine and liquor shop).

nana

organic breakfast and lunch

3267 South Halsted Street
Corner of 33rd (Bridgeport) *map E45*
CTA Bus: 8
312.929.2486
www.nanaorganic.com

twitter @nanaorganic
mon - thu 9a - 9p fri 9a - 10p
sat 8a - 10p sun 8a - 9p
$-$$ first come, first served

Yes, Please: *fresh squeezed beet juice, liege waffle, banana hemp cakes, mascarpone stuffed french toast, magic mushroom burger, heirloom tart apple salad, patty melt*

Menus change, dishes come and go, but for all of our sakes, I sincerely hope that the banana hemp pancakes on **Nana**'s menu never go away. They are simply more delicious than any pancakes you could make at home, and considering the family affair of Omar and Chris Solis and their mother Nana, who is always in the kitchen, it isn't surprising that the food here tastes homemade. Add in that everything on this menu is organic and as local as can be, and you may never eat breakfast or lunch at your own home again.

optimo hats

custom hat maker

10215 South Western Avenue
Between 103rd and 102nd
(South Side) *map S34*
Metrarail: 103rd
773.238.2999
www.optimohats.com

mon - sat 10a - 6p
custom orders

Yes, Please: *hats: montecristi panama straw, milan straw, the manhattan, the classic fedora, trilby, the traveler, the adventurer, the rush street, the seville*

It's hard to find fine craftsmen in this country because they keep getting replaced by machines and conveyer belts. Let me therefore introduce you to **Optimo Hats**. Graham Thompson, the owner, is a true craftsman who brings skill, finesse and enormous attention to detail in his hat-making. He uses equipment from the South of France, travels to Ecuador for supplies to make the Montecristi straw hat and sources ribbons in Europe. If all this doesn't turn you into an **Optimo** hat-wearer, I don't know what will.

pleasant house bakery
savory royal pie shop

964 West 31st Street
Corner of Morgan (Bridgeport) *map E46*
CTA Bus: 62
7773.523.7437
www.pleasanthousebakery.com

twitter @phbakery
tue - thu 11a - 9p fri - sat 11a - 10p
sun noon - 8p
lunch, dinner, byob
$ first come, first served

Yes, Please: *housemade spicy ginger ale, deluxe gravy chips, peas buttered with mint; royal pies: steak & ale, mushroom & kale, chicken balti*

Fifty years ago or so, just about everyone knew or was related to a farmer. Now it's gotten to be a rare thing to know a farmer, let alone to know someone who knows a farmer. Thanks to the people at **Pleasant House Farm**, times are a-changin'. **Pleasant House Bakery** grows a good portion of the ingredients they use on different plots around the neighborhood, with a full-time farmer on hand to compost, weed and harvest. Now, not only will you know where to get tasty savory royal pies, but you will also have bragging rights to having a farmer friend.

zap. props & antiques

fabulous miscellany for rent

3641 South Loomis Place
Off of 37th (South Side) *map S35*
CTA Bus #35: Iron Street
773.376.2278
www.zapprops.com

mon - thu 9a - 5p fri 8a - 3p
rentals. design services

Yes, Please: *for rent: telephones, typewriters, factory signs, diner decor, general store items, mid-century mod tvs, frames & framing services*

Please don't get too attached to any of the items you see in these photos: it's more than likely that you can't buy them. You can, however, rent them. I know, I know, I'm pushing it—this isn't a book about rentals, but I was so wowed by this place I wanted to spread the word. Though **Zap Props** does have a selection of for-sale items, the bulk of the stuff here is for borrowing only. While I don't know why you might want to rent a clown, an old telephone, or a Coca-Cola sign, I'm pretty sure you creative types out there will think of something.

finito

happy travels to you

rather *chicago*

isbn-13 9780983314530

copyright 2011 ©swiftrank. printed in the usa

every effort has been made to ensure the accuracy of the information in this book. however, certain details are subject to change. please remember when using the guides that hours alter seasonally and sometimes sadly, businesses close. the publisher cannot accept responsibility for any consequences arising from the use of this book.

editing / fact checking + production: chloe fields
in design master: nicole conant
map design + production: bryan wolf

thx to our friends at designers & agents for their hospitality and their support of the rather experience. please visit > designersandagents.com

rather is distributed by
independent publishers group > www.ipgbook.com

to peer further into the world of **rather** and to buy books, please visit **rather.com** to learn more